spot

ARCTIC ANIMALS

POLAR BEARS

by Anastasia Suen

AMICUS | AMICUS INK

claws

eyes

Look for these
words and pictures
as you read.

nose

fur

What is swimming in the sea?
It is a polar bear.

Polar bears live in the Arctic.
They are sea bears.

See the nose?

It sniffs out seals.

It can smell under the ice.

nose

eyes

See the eyes?

They stay open in the water.

They look for seals to eat.

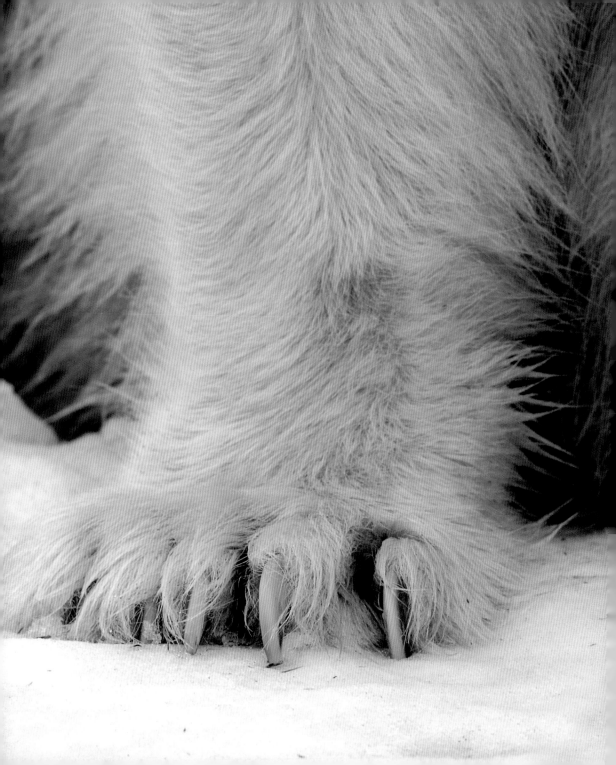

See the claws?
They are sharp.
They grab food.

claws

fur

See the thick fur?

It repels water.

It keeps the bear dry.

Polar bears have cubs.
The cubs follow mom.

See the claws?
They are sharp.
They grab food.

claws

eyes

See the eyes?
They stay open in the water.
They look for seals to eat.

eyes

Did you find?

nose

See the nose?
It sniffs out seals.
It can smell under the ice.

nose

fur

fur

See the thick fur?
It repels water.
It keeps the bear dry.

spot

Spot is published by Amicus and Amicus Ink
P.O. Box 1329, Mankato, MN 56002
www.amicuspublishing.us

Library of Congress Cataloging-in-Publication Data
Names: Suen, Anastasia, author.
Title: Polar bears / by Anastasia Suen.
Description: Mankato, Minnesota : Amicus/Amicus Ink,
   [2020] | Series: Spot arctic animals | Audience: K to
   Grade 3.
Identifiers: LCCN 2018047346 (print) | LCCN 2018048387
   (ebook) | ISBN 9781681518374 (pdf) | ISBN
   9781681517971 (library binding) | ISBN 9781681525259
   (paperback)
Subjects: LCSH: Polar bear—Juvenile literature.
Classification: LCC QL737.C27 (ebook) | LCC QL737.C27
   S84 2020 (print) | DDC 599.786—dc23
LC record available at https://lccn.loc.gov/2018047346

Printed in China

HC 10 9 8 7 6 5 4 3 2 1
PB 10 9 8 7 6 5 4 3 2 1

Alissa Thielges, editor
Deb Miner, series designer
Ciara Beitlich, book designer
Holly Young and Shane Freed,
   photo researchers

Photos by SuperStock/Steven Kazlowski
cover, 16; iStock/gnagel 1; Shutterstock/
Nagel Photography 3; Alamy/Paul
Souders 4–5; iStock/dagsjo 6–7; iStock/
sarkophoto 8–9; Nat Geo Creative/Ira
Meyer 10–11; Alamy/Pat Kerrigan 12–
13; Getty/Thorsten Milse/robertharding
14–15

POLAR BEARS